I Am
Cleopatra

By Grace Norwich

Illustrated by
Elisabeth Alba

SCHOLASTIC INC.

PHOTO CREDITS

Photographs © 2014: Courtesy of Barnes & Noble: 25; Getty Images: 1 main, 20 (DEA Picture Library), 78 (Werner Forman/Universal Images Group); Shutterstock, Inc.: 10 (Jose Ignacio Soto), 108 (josefbosak), papyrus background throughout (Nancy Nehring), 48 top (Perytskyy), 19 (Photoservice); Shutterstock, Inc.: 28 bottom (Africa Studio), 29 (Elzbieta Sekowska), 58 center (FooTToo), 16 (Frontpage), 48 bottom (GTS Production), 34 (jsp), 39 (Marina Plug), 28 center (Nattika), 50, 58 bottom (pseudolongino), 30 (S. Borisov), 28 top (Tamara Kulikova); Shutterstock, Inc.: 70 (FooTToo), The Granger Collection/DEA Picture Library: 73; Thinkstock: 48 center (Hemera), 40, 58 top, 82, 104 (iStockphoto).

ISBN 978-0-545-58753-2

10 9 8 7 6 5 4   14 15 16 17 18 19/0

Printed in the U.S.A.   40
First printing, January 2014

Cover illustration by Mark Fredrickson
Interior illustrations by Elisabeth Alba
Book design by Kay Petronio

CONTENTS

INTRODUCTION

There have been many powerful women throughout history, including empresses and queens, presidents and prime ministers. They have all been great in their own way, and I welcome them into the sisterhood of leading ladies. But were any more powerful than me? I think not. After all, my decades-long reign came during a time of enormous violence and disorder.

For all my many accomplishments, much focus has been given to my beauty. While it's true that I had an attractive oval-shaped face, dark hair, and honey-colored skin, I did not get by on looks alone. My charm, charisma, and wit were just as important to my rise to power, if not more so. I was one of the sharpest rulers of ancient Egypt, with a sense for knowing what people wanted before they knew it themselves.

Some have called me manipulative. To them, I say, "All is fair in love and war." And I should know, given the number of battles I fought and romances I enjoyed throughout my thirty-nine years.

I even made sure my death occurred on my own terms, rather than letting someone else take my life. And as you're about to read, history has judged me favorably, calling me one of the most dynamic figures—male or female—that the world has ever known.

I am Cleopatra.

PEOPLE YOU WILL MEET

CLEOPATRA
The last pharaoh of ancient Egypt, she ruled for nineteen years.

....

Alexander the Great: One of the most powerful warriors of all time, he created one of the largest **empires** of the ancient world.

Ptolemy I: A general in Alexander the Great's army who was given the rule of Egypt as a reward for his service and loyalty.

Ptolemy XII: Cleopatra's father, from whom she would inherit the throne.

Berenice IV: Cleopatra's older sister, who was executed by their father after she attempted to take control of Egypt.

Ptolemy XIII: Cleopatra's younger brother, with whom she once shared the throne, before a sibling split resulted in war and ultimately his death.

Arsinoe: Cleopatra's younger sister and long-time rival for power.

Julius Caesar: The Roman general and statesman who was assassinated by his own people. He and Cleopatra were romantically involved.

Mark Antony: A Roman general and politician, known for his bravery and ambition as well as for his relationship with Cleopatra.

Octavian: Caesar's great-nephew and adopted son, who took over the Roman Empire after Caesar's murder and helped bring about Cleopatra's demise.

TIME LINE

323 BCE
Alexander the Great dies and his empire is divided into three parts, with ancient Egypt going to his trusted adviser Ptolemy I.

69 BCE
Cleopatra is born to Ptolemy XII, a descendant of Ptolemy I, and an unknown woman.

51 BCE
Following the death of their father, Cleopatra and her younger brother Ptolemy XIII take over the throne.

49 BCE
Ptolemy XIII and his advisers force Cleopatra into exile. She raises an army and marches on Alexandria to take the throne back.

47 BCE
After winning the Alexandrian War, Julius Caesar makes Cleopatra the ruler of Egypt.

46 BCE
Cleopatra travels to Rome with her son and her brother Ptolemy XIV.

MARCH 15, 44 BCE
Caesar is murdered on the steps of the Roman Senate.

41 BCE
Cleopatra and Mark Antony begin their legendary romance, marked by luxury and adventure.

40 BCE
Cleopatra gives birth to twins, Alexander Helios and Cleopatra Selene.

AUGUST 1, 30 BCE
Mark Antony takes his own life, using a sword.

AUGUST 12, 30 BCE
Cleopatra takes her own life by drinking a deadly poison.

BCE TIME
BCE stands for "Before the Common Era." It measures time before our modern calendar began. BCE dates are like a countdown, so they go backward. The biggest numbers are the oldest dates, and the smallest numbers are closest to the present time.

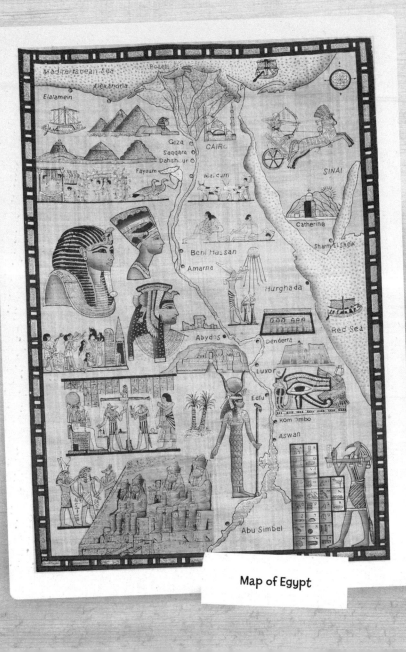

Map of Egypt

CHAPTER ONE

PORTRAIT OF THE ANCIENT WORLD

To appreciate the life of Cleopatra, it is important to first understand the world in which she lived. That requires traveling back in time more than two thousand years to a place known as ancient Egypt. At this point in history, humans had developed civilizations throughout the world.

But ancient Egypt, which was located in present-day Northeast Africa, was one of the most important civilizations of its time. That's largely due to the actions of one man: Alexander the Great, a mighty warrior who created one of the largest empires of the ancient world after taking over the throne of Macedon in 336 BCE. Macedon was a northern kingdom in ancient Greece.

When Alexander died in 323 BCE, his sprawling empire was divided into three parts. A man named Ptolemy, who had been a general in Alexander's army and one of his closest advisers, was given the part of the empire known as Egypt. As a distant relative of Ptolemy, many generations removed, Cleopatra would later benefit from this arrangement.

Like Alexander, Ptolemy was Greek, but he immediately declared himself pharaoh, the title given to Egyptian kings. He did not, however, give up the Greek culture, religion, or even its language. He made sure that the growing capital city—named Alexandria after Alexander the Great—adopted Greece's way of life.

Alexandria the Great

Fast-forward two hundred and fifty years, around the year 75 BCE, and Alexandria was the largest port city in the world. Its two harbors on the Nile

Alexander the Great

River could each hold twelve hundred ships at once, and traders, scholars, and sailors from all over the world visited, bringing knowledge and goods from Greece, Italy, Asia, and other regions of Africa.

The city of Alexandria

Alexandria even outshone the Italian city of Rome in terms of population, history, and culture. Its three hundred thousand citizens were made up of many different groups. The Greeks, the powerful ruling class, lived in the middle of the city, nearest the Great Harbor. They never adjusted to the native Egyptian culture, despite ruling it for hundreds of years. The Egyptian community lived on the west side and was considered second class.

Alexandria was a beautiful, wealthy city. The main streets were paved and lit by torches at night. Many of the buildings were made of marble, and there were sculptures and statues everywhere. The city was colorful, hung with silk awnings, and the air was filled with perfumes and spices of all kinds.

There's one final detail of Alexandria that would prove particularly significant for Cleopatra: The women from this society had

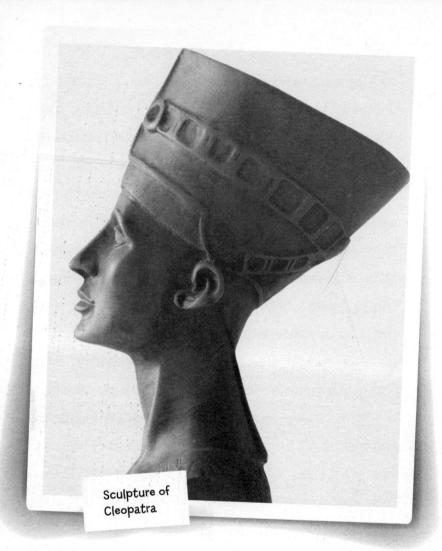

Sculpture of Cleopatra

power and status. Unlike most women in the ancient world, Egyptian women could inherit and own property independent of male relatives.

They could arrange their own marriages and, once married, they were not under their husbands' control. They could manage their own business affairs whether or not they were married and could serve as priests in local temples.

All in all, ancient Egypt was a rather splendid place to live, especially if you were lucky enough to be born into the Greek ruling class. If you also happened to be a woman with great charm and ambition, it was even better.

The ancient Egyptians used a writing system of symbols called hieroglyphs. This is how Cleopatra's name looks written in Egyptian hieroglyphs:

The Nile River: Source of Ancient Prosperity

The Nile River was essential to life and economic success throughout ancient Egypt, including in the port city of Alexandria. Egypt is a desert country, but water from the Nile creates long strips of green land on either side of the river. During the rainy season, the river would flood, sending water out over the shallow valley. When these waters receded, a layer of dense, fertile soil was left behind. Egypt's farmers were able to grow all kinds of fruits and vegetables, including grapes for making wine, and huge quantities of wheat. These products were used in Egypt and also sold to other countries, which is why the Nile was so important to the wealth of ancient Egypt.

Sculpture of Cleopatra

CHAPTER TWO

A PRINCESS IS BORN

In the year 69 BCE, about two hundred and fifty years after Ptolemy I became pharaoh of Egypt, his direct descendant, Ptolemy XII, announced the birth of a daughter. Her name was Cleopatra. While the identity of her mother is unknown, some historians believe she may have been Ptolemy XII's sister-wife Cleopatra Tryphaeana. It was common for siblings to marry each other and have children together during ancient times.

Cleopatra as a baby

Though Cleopatra was certainly fortunate to be born a princess, the city of Alexandria and its ruling family (known as the Ptolemies) were both falling on hard times. The last few generations of Ptolemies that came before Cleopatra had not been very skilled at managing the empire.

Still, her family's declining power didn't have any noticeable effects on the life of young Cleopatra or her siblings. She had an older sister named Berenice, a younger sister named Arsinoe, and two younger brothers who are now known only as Ptolemy XIII and Ptolemy XIV.

Cleopatra's Daily Life

As a young child, Cleopatra played with dolls made of clay and wood, miniature cups, and doll furniture, as well as balls, dice, and board games. Her father was known by the name Auletes, meaning "the flute player." He was a musician and patron of the arts in Alexandria.

The Ptolemies followed Egyptian law, which stated that women could inherit the throne of Egypt, ruling alone or as co-rulers alongside husbands or brothers. As a result, Cleopatra and her sisters were given the best education possible. Cleopatra and her siblings were able to study at Alexandria's library and its museum.

But privilege had its cost. In ancient times, children, even those born into royalty, were disciplined severely if their attention wandered. They were punished if they answered questions incorrectly.

And the lessons were difficult. Even very young students were expected to memorize fables, stories, and lists of gods and heroes. As they got older, they would have to read entire sections of very complicated and dense books like *The Iliad* and *The Odyssey*, both written by the ancient Greek poet Homer. Reading aloud was common, and when she was in her early teens, Cleopatra was taught the art of public speaking, which is essential for a ruler who needs the approval of her subjects. She also learned—from her family's history and studies of current events—how dangerous

Cleopatra studied books by Homer.

it was to be on Rome's bad side.

Even with the fear of Rome present in her mind, Cleopatra probably didn't worry about her future. The Egyptian religion gave the pharaohs and the royal family godlike status. That meant that as the daughter of a pharaoh, Cleopatra and her siblings were considered the children of a god.

Daily life for Cleopatra was similar to that of any well-born Greek or Roman girl, though her surroundings were even more extravagant. She wore jewelry and makeup from a young age. She went barefoot while indoors, wearing floor-length, soft, sleeveless dresses of linen or silk with long robes over them. Outside she wore sandals made of cork, or shoes made of dyed leather. For state affairs, even from the time she was a teenager, she dressed in traditional Egyptian garments designed to make her look like popular depictions of the Egyptian goddess Isis.

Clever Cleopatra

Cleopatra's plan to appear like Isis was one of the first signs of her political cleverness. In the Egyptian religion, Isis was the wife of Osiris, god of the underworld and the dead. She was associated with agriculture, fertility, and loyalty. An Egyptian religious **myth** says that when Osiris's brother killed him, he cut him into fourteen pieces and threw them all into the Nile River. Isis searched for years until she found all the pieces and put her husband back together.

Throughout the Mediterranean, including the city of Rome, Isis was seen as the renewer of life, despite great difficulties. Identifying herself with that message was a wise political move for Cleopatra.

The decision became all the more important as her family's power continued to weaken. In 58 BCE, when Cleopatra was eleven years old, the Alexandrians revolted against high taxes and Rome's increasing authority over Egyptian affairs. Cleopatra's father had no option but to ask for protection from Rome against his own citizens, who drove him out of Egypt. Ptolemy XII fled to Rome for safety.

A Meal Fit for a Queen

Egypt was an agricultural powerhouse, thanks to the Nile River. Given that Cleopatra was royalty, her meal options were endless and included pork and chicken, plus more unusual offerings such as porcupine, quail, and gazelle. She also ate garlic, onion, cheese, beans, lentils, cucumbers, lettuce, eggs, and plenty of bread. Alexandria was a port city, so nearly every kind of fish and shellfish was available. All people ate with their hands, although royalty ate off of plates made of silver and gold. Sometimes bread was used as a plate, or even a napkin. Desserts included grapes, figs, and honey cakes.

Fertile farmland
on the banks of
the Nile River

The ruins of the
Roman Forum

CHAPTER THREE

POWER STRUGGLES

While not much is known about Cleopatra's father, one thing is fairly certain: He was not a very good ruler of Egypt. In fact, he managed to waste most of the state's money. Despite his failings as a ruler, Cleopatra is thought to have had a soft spot for her father, and he was apparently devoted to her as well. It must have been very difficult for Cleopatra to see him fail.

Once Ptolemy XII was driven out of Alexandria, Cleopatra's older sister, Berenice IV, wasted no time taking control of the government. By this point, Cleopatra was probably well aware of her family's ruthless, backstabbing ways, but her sister's action still might have come as a shock.

Power Struggles

Berenice was popular with the Alexandrians, so she thought she would become an effective leader. But the fact that she wasn't married complicated her situation. Even though Egyptian women could rule alone, they usually had a co-ruler. No one knows why Berenice didn't just marry to solve the problem, but the people of Alexandria didn't like that she was single, and so they chose a foreign-born prince for her. Unfortunately, she didn't much care for the prince, and she had him strangled a few days after the marriage. Her next husband, Archelaus, a priest who didn't like Rome, suited her better, and they ruled jointly for the next three years.

Cleopatra had a front-row seat to all of the betrayals and murders going on in her family. During the period when her sister ruled Egypt, nothing is known about what Cleopatra did, which probably means she continued her studies and stayed out of the spotlight.

Cleopatra was very smart, and even from her early teens it's clear that she had her eye on long-term goals. She wanted the Egyptian people to like her. She wanted to become their queen. Probably with that goal in mind, Cleopatra learned to speak Egyptian. She was the only member of her family to do so. Even more than her decision to take on the public persona of Isis, this act won over the native Egyptians.

The people must have also been impressed by her intellect. Cleopatra could speak nine

Ancient Egyptian hieroglyphs

languages, which was a huge advantage, especially in the large port city of Alexandria.

Cleopatra must have known that becoming the ruler of Egypt was a very real possibility. There were many women in the Ptolemaic family who had wielded power, including her older sister. When Berenice's power over Alexandria became weak, Cleopatra saw that she could seize the throne for herself. Berenice's days as the ruler of Egypt were numbered.

Berenice and Cleopatra's father, Ptolemy XII, had gained enough support from Rome to organize an army to seize Alexandria back from his daughter. Leading the cavalry was a young man named Mark Antony, who fought bravely against the Alexandrians. For those in Alexandria who had remained loyal to the pharaoh while he had been away in Rome—like the fourteen-year-old princess, Cleopatra—Mark Antony was seen as a hero.

The Roman army quickly overpowered the Alexandrians, Alexandria fell quickly, and Berenice's husband was killed in battle. Ptolemy XII had his daughter Berenice executed for her crimes against him; the major crime was **treason**.

Mark Antony led
the cavalry.

He then wrote his will, naming Cleopatra and her six-year-old brother, Ptolemy XIII, as his **successors**. They would be next in line to the throne. Ptolemy XII wanted to guarantee that his family would continue to rule. He probably also wanted to protect Cleopatra from further power struggles by giving her a strong marriage within the family right away. Marrying Cleopatra to her brother would keep power within the family.

Ptolemy XII died of natural causes in 51 BCE. It's likely that Cleopatra had been brought into the daily business of ruling the empire during the last months of her father's life. By the time eighteen-year-old Cleopatra and Ptolemy XIII took the throne together, she was in command— and not about to let her ten-year-old brother tell her what to do. Unlike most of her ancestors, she was prepared to take over the throne and the country. That's a good thing, because she was about to inherit a very messy situation.

Sibling Marriages: All in the Family

The royal families of ancient Egypt married within their own families. They believed that they were descended from the gods themselves. Since the gods and goddesses in myth married their siblings, so too did the pharaohs. Greek religious myths were full of brother-sister relationships. Zeus, the powerful father of the gods and of men, was married to his sister, Hera. In the case of Cleopatra and her much younger brother Ptolemy XIII, their marriage was a way to consolidate the family power. Their marriage was also a way to honor the gods and keep the Ptolemy bloodline pure.

This Greek temple was built to honor Zeus.

The Nile River
in Egypt

CHAPTER FOUR

CLEOPATRA'S ROCKY EARLY REIGN

Once Cleopatra took the throne, she continued her campaign to win over the Egyptian people. It's important to remember that Cleopatra wasn't actually Egyptian by birth. Because of this, she felt strongly that in order to maintain power, she would have to identify herself more with the Egyptian population. The Alexandrians had betrayed her father and driven him from the throne. They could do the same to her so she appealed to the Egyptians outside of Alexandria.

A few weeks after her father's death, Cleopatra took a trip to the ancient Egyptian city of Thebes with the royal fleet. The purpose of the journey was to participate in a religious ceremony. While in Thebes, she also declared herself a goddess. This was a powerful act to the Egyptian people, who worshipped gods and goddesses. Her title

Cleopatra travels to Thebes.

as queen was Cleopatra VII Philopator, Lady of the Two Lands.

Philopator means "she who loves her father." We know that Cleopatra and Ptolemy XII had been close, but as with most things Cleopatra did, this move had a political message. It was a reminder to the Alexandrians that she was the daughter of the pharaoh—the man they had betrayed. The second part of her title, Lady of the Two Lands, referred to Cleopatra's power over Upper and Lower Egypt, and the seven million native Egyptians who lived there.

And what about Cleopatra's younger brother and co-ruler? At least in the beginning, it seems Ptolemy XIII was not involved in ruling the country. In fact, the money made during the first year of the siblings' joint reign had only Cleopatra's face on it. There is no mention of her younger brother, which probably suited Cleopatra just fine.

However, by 49 BCE, the balance of power had shifted toward Ptolemy XIII's team of advisers. Ptolemy was barely twelve years old and would have been easily controlled by the elder statesmen. They knew that the brilliant, capable Cleopatra was a constant threat to their own power, and so they managed to force her out.

Queen Cleopatra's Early Years

Some of Cleopatra's loss of control during the early period of her reign was the result of natural causes. The Nile didn't flood for the first two years of Cleopatra and Ptolemy XIII's reign. That was a problem since the flood waters were necessary to make the soil suitable for farming. Because Cleopatra was the more visible ruler, she took a lot of the blame. As a goddess she was supposed to be able to prevent such things. Without crops to feed them, and **famine** a real possibility, the Alexandrians began to consider an open rebellion against the country's rulers. Ptolemy XIII's advisers started rumors blaming Cleopatra for the crisis. Cleopatra knew she couldn't do anything about it, and public opinion was starting to turn against her. So she fled the capital city and took safe **refuge** in the desert.

With Cleopatra out of the picture, her seventeen-year-old sister, Arsinoe, started becoming friendly with Ptolemy XIII's general, Achillas. It seemed the Ptolemy family's double-crossing ways were alive and well. The family members constantly competed for power.

History prepared Cleopatra for this turn of events. She fled to the deserts of Syria and started raising an army. Her skill with languages was a huge advantage. While recruiting a **mercenary** army in Syria, she could speak to the Syrians and Medians in their own languages. It helped that she was only twenty-one years old, incredibly persuasive, and good-looking.

The army Cleopatra raised worried Ptolemy XIII and his advisers enough that they sent their own troops out to meet her at Pelusium, a fortress by the Mediterranean Sea. His army included twenty thousand rough soldiers including bandits, outlaws, exiles, and fugitive slaves.

The situation was further complicated by a civil war, which was taking place in Rome between two men and their armies. Julius Caesar and Pompey the Great were both powerful Roman generals who each wanted complete control of Rome. Caesar won the war, defeating Pompey in August 48 BCE. Pompey had always been an ally and protector of Cleopatra's father, and so when he was defeated in the civil war with Caesar, he decided to flee to Egypt.

Julius Caesar

Ptolemy XIII's advisers couldn't agree on what to do about Pompey. To give him refuge would anger Rome, something no Egyptian monarch could afford to do. And once he was in Egypt, he might back Cleopatra, whom he already liked. Eventually, Ptolemy XIII's tutor and adviser Theodotus made the recommendation that Pompey simply be killed. A message of welcome and a boat were sent to Pompey's ship, and Ptolemy XIII watched from the beach as Pompey was killed before he ever made it to shore.

Even though Cleopatra probably wasn't surprised at what happened, it must have made her feel more **vulnerable**. If her army didn't succeed against her brother's, she knew she would probably be killed like Pompey. She needed a Roman leader with an army on her side.

Luckily, she got one.

What Did Cleopatra Look Like?

There are no reliable paintings or drawings of Cleopatra. But we do know that her beauty has been exaggerated through the ages. Ancient historians agree that she was good-looking but not absolutely gorgeous. She had an oval face and large, wide-set eyes. She was also small in stature, and likely had dark hair and honey-colored skin.

But while Cleopatra's looks are up for debate, the way she spoke and carried herself added to her beauty. The culture of the time was an oral one, and Cleopatra spoke superbly. According to historians, she was blessed with "sparkling eyes," as well as "eloquence and charisma," a "commanding presence," and a "rich, velvety voice." Being one of the wealthiest women in the world probably didn't hurt either!

A statue of
Julius Caesar

CHAPTER FIVE

CLEOPATRA'S GAMBLE

Julius Caesar was right behind his defeated rival. Three days after Pompey's murder, Caesar arrived in Egypt. Most of his troops hadn't arrived yet. He wore the imperial red of an emperor of Rome, which made the already anxious Alexandrians concerned that he was about to take over their country. When Caesar reached the palace, Theodotus tried to give him Pompey's severed head. The victorious Roman general turned away and burst into tears, though most historians believe Caesar's show of grief over the death of his former rival was all an act.

Caesar immediately took over a section of the Ptolemies' palace. The Alexandrians were rioting against him, and he sent for reinforcements at once. Meanwhile, in the wake of Pompey's murder and Caesar's arrival, Ptolemy XIII had run off to be with his army at Pelusium. Pothinus, a former servant of the young king and one of his closest advisers, went quickly to Pelusium to bring the young king back from his standoff with Cleopatra's troops.

Even though Pompey no longer posed a threat to Caesar, his supporters were still active in the Roman Senate, so Caesar decided to remain in Alexandria. In a letter home he blamed the weather, claiming that he was stuck in Egypt because of "prevailing northwest winds." He didn't want to admit the real reason, which was that Egypt was a very rich country, and Caesar wanted cash to secure his military and political strength. But it became clear that Caesar would have to settle the political situation between Cleopatra and Ptolemy XIII one way or another if he wanted any of Egypt's support and riches.

Caesar summoned Cleopatra and Ptolemy XIII to help them work out their differences. Cleopatra couldn't risk bringing her army into Egypt as long as Ptolemy's army was standing in the way at Pelusium, but she couldn't hide out for much longer. Every day she didn't appear to plead her own case in the feud with her brother was another day that Ptolemy's advisers had to get Caesar on their side. Cleopatra had to think of a plan—and fast.

Ptolemy in hieroglyphs

A Royal Plan

Clever Cleopatra hatched a plan that involved one of her most loyal friends, a man named Apollodorus. Traveling in disguise, the two made their way up the Nile and then back along the coast to Alexandria. All this time, Ptolemy's advisers were stalling and keeping Ptolemy

Cleopatra and Apollodorus travel up the Nile River.

from returning to his palace in Alexandria to meet with Caesar. Ptolemy's adviser Pothinus didn't want Ptolemy and Cleopatra to reconcile, and he also wanted Rome out of Egypt's affairs.

Meanwhile, a tiny, two-oared boat snuck into the Great Harbor at Alexandria. While Apollodorus rowed, Cleopatra got into a large sack, made of either hemp or leather. It was the kind of thing usually used to transfer gold or rolls of papyrus. Apollodorus secured the sack with a leather cord and slung it—gently!—over his shoulder. He set out through the grounds of the palace where Cleopatra had grown up. It was a beautiful place, the floors intricately tiled in mosaics in some places, and made of black onyx in others. Apollodorus carried Cleopatra over his shoulder through the palace's gardens, finally delivering her to Caesar's rooms, which technically still belonged to her as one of Egypt's rulers.

It wasn't easy to surprise the fifty-two-year-old Caesar, but Cleopatra managed it. The drama of the moment wasn't lost on either of them; they had both been raised in the same theatrical culture. After the initial shock of seeing a young woman appear before him out

Cleopatra surprises Caesar.

of a sack, no one really knows what happened next.

Cleopatra had sided with Pompey against Caesar in the Roman civil war, and so she had some negotiating to do with the Roman general. But she was confident that she could impress him. Despite her youth, she had already been a goddess-queen, been **exiled**, and had raised an army to help her win back the throne. She had also just put herself completely in Caesar's power. If he wanted to side with her brother, all he needed to do was kill her, and she'd presented him with an easy opportunity to do just that.

Portrait of Julius Caesar

What made Caesar so powerful? For one thing, he liked traveling fast. He often rode ahead of his own troops, a signal that he meant to fight himself, instead of just leaving it to others. He also made decisions quickly, and liked to rely on his own judgment of people. Caesar was also brave. When Sulla, Rome's dictator when Caesar was a young man, demanded that Caesar divorce his wife or else face execution, Caesar refused. He joined the army and left Rome until after Sulla's death. He rose up the military and political ranks quickly. Pompey, fearing Caesar's wealth and power, used his own power as head of the Roman Senate to try to order Caesar to come back to Rome without his army, but Caesar refused. In short, he was the kind of man who took orders from no one.

Cleopatra

CHAPTER SIX

CLEOPATRA CHARMS CAESAR

I t is not known exactly what was said between Cleopatra and Caesar that night, but he was clearly impressed by the young woman. She made a strong case that she should be queen of Egypt and Caesar agreed.

Caesar declared that Ptolemy and Cleopatra should reconcile as long as Cleopatra was allowed to maintain her status as co-ruler. Ptolemy's advisers were shocked by Caesar's declaration, since they believed they had the

Throne in hieroglyphs

upper hand, controlling both Ptolemy and Caesar. When Ptolemy XIII heard the news, he ran through the palace gates and into the crowd on the street, crying that Cleopatra had betrayed him. Caesar's men grabbed him and got him back inside, where they kept him under house arrest.

The Alexandrians rioted and Caesar's men had trouble putting a stop to the violence. Pothinus, Ptolemy's adviser, encouraged the rioting and rebellion, thinking he might be able to kick the Romans out and remove Cleopatra at the same time. Caesar didn't have a very good understanding of Alexandrian politics, but he learned fast. He gave a compelling speech to the Alexandrian people—most likely from one

of the palace's upper windows or balconies—
in which he promised that he would do what
the people wanted. It's possible that Cleopatra
counseled him on what to say to her people.

A Royal Reunion

Ptolemy XIII agreed to rule with his sister
even though he was probably counting on his
advisers to keep him in power. At that point they
were secretly bringing Ptolemy's army back to
Alexandria to fight Caesar's soldiers.

At a formal assembly, Cleopatra and Ptolemy
XIII stood together with Caesar as he read their
father's will aloud. He announced that Ptolemy
XII had clearly wanted the two siblings to
rule together under Roman guardianship and
friendship, and he presented them with their
kingdom. Additionally, he gave the island of
Cyprus to the remaining two siblings, Arsinoe
and Ptolemy XIV.

Though the will was clear, reading it aloud didn't actually solve the problem. There was still a war taking place between Ptolemy's and Caesar's armies. Ptolemy's advisers had to get Caesar out of Egypt so that they could remain in power. In October, Ptolemy XIII's general, Achillas, led Ptolemy's army into Alexandria. Caesar refused to leave. He made his headquarters in the palace to protect the royal family as the fighting between Ptolemy's army and Caesar's soldiers flared up around them.

The Alexandrian War

The battle would come to be known as the Alexandrian War. It went on for months, until Caesar's reinforcements finally arrived in Egypt. Caesar led his men in a sneak attack against Ptolemy's camp. They pushed his army back to the Nile, and Ptolemy himself drowned in the river during the final battle.

The Alexandrian War

The war came to a sudden end. On March 27, 47 BCE, Caesar led his troops on a parade through Alexandria, displaying Ptolemy's **gilded** armor as a symbol of Caesar's victory over him. The people begged Caesar for mercy, bowing down in front of him, and Caesar granted it. He had his eye on the prize, which was Egypt's great wealth. He wanted a stable government in Egypt that was friendly to Rome, and he had personal reasons for wanting that government to involve Cleopatra.

Caesar had the opportunity, as the conqueror of Alexandria, to take Egypt as part of the Roman Republic, but this option came with some problems. If he officially made Egypt part of the Roman Empire, he would need to appoint someone to control it, and whoever controlled Egypt would have unlimited access to its vast treasury and resources. That person could then raise a huge army and threaten Caesar's own power, not to mention challenge Rome directly. Caesar decided it was better to leave Cleopatra in charge.

With the war over, Caesar forgave all his—and Cleopatra's—enemies, except Cleopatra's remaining sister, Arsinoe. He had her sent to Rome as a prisoner. He wanted to get her out of the way because she had proven she couldn't be trusted. Cleopatra married her only remaining brother, the twelve-year-old Ptolemy XIV, and resumed the throne, basically ruling alone once again. Caesar ought to have gone back to Rome, but he remained in Egypt, where he and Cleopatra had a romantic relationship even though Caesar had a wife back in Rome.

Just after the end of the war, Cleopatra and Caesar took a cruise up the Nile in the royal barge. They were accompanied by four hundred vessels of different sizes. The couple viewed the pyramids and the many impressive temples lining the Nile. They were adored

Cleopatra and Caesar travel the Nile together.

wherever they went. Cleopatra used this trip for political as well as personal reasons. She had always been popular with the native Egyptian people, and this was a chance to display herself as powerful and divine once again after her exile and the war.

At this point, Cleopatra was pregnant. Cleopatra proclaimed Caesar the father of her child, and Caesar never denied it.

But Caesar's time in Egypt with Cleopatra had to come to an end. Caesar had to return to Rome and to his wife, Calpurnia. He departed Egypt in May 47 BCE, leaving an army made up of three **legions** to protect the Ptolemies and keep the peace. On June 23, Cleopatra gave birth to a son. She named him Ptolemy Caesar, but called him Caesarion, meaning "Little Caesar."

Statue of
Julius Caesar

CHAPTER SEVEN

THE BETRAYAL OF CAESAR

Cleopatra and Ptolemy XIV traveled to Rome along with Caesarion in 46 BCE. In September, Caesar's victories in many different places were being celebrated in Rome. It is possible that Cleopatra was there for those celebrations, which included a parade of Caesar's war prizes. Caesar was last in the parade, with torches carried by forty elephants lighting the way.

Arsinoe was also in the parade. She was led

through the streets, covered in chains, as one of the prisoners of war. Many Romans were quite sympathetic toward the young princess. They were impressed by her dignity as she was paraded through the streets. They wanted mercy for her and Caesar agreed to spare her life.

Roman Politics

But the Romans weren't sure how to react to Cleopatra. Part of this was because Caesar made little effort to hide the true nature of his relationship with Cleopatra. He gave the queen a villa on his own estate in a wealthy part of the city. There are few recorded details of Cleopatra's time in Rome, but there were rumors that Caesar planned to pass a law that would make it possible for him to have two wives. He also wanted to recognize Caesarion as his heir in Rome (foreigners could not inherit Roman property at the time), and he wanted to declare himself king and rule as a god.

Roman culture was much more conservative than Alexandrian culture. Romans were put off by the luxuries and gifts Caesar was providing the Egyptian queen, and they blamed Cleopatra for Caesar's behavior. She was also a powerful woman in a society that did not appreciate powerful women. Women in Rome supported

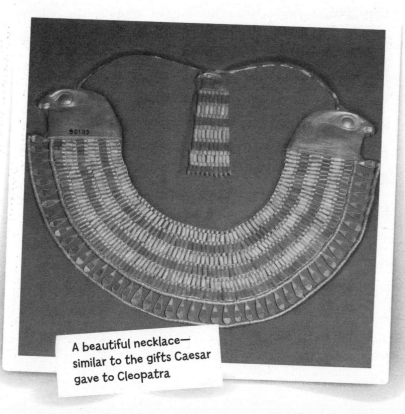

A beautiful necklace— similar to the gifts Caesar gave to Cleopatra

their husbands' political careers, but they did not participate in politics.

Despite the difficulties she faced, it seemed that Cleopatra's stay in Rome was having good results for her politically. Caesar publicly renewed the pact that had been made with her father, declaring her a friend and ally of Rome.

Even though there were rumors that Cleopatra had too much influence on him, Caesar was very popular with his people as well. His military victories were the most impressive in the history of Rome, and in 44 BCE, the Roman Senate acknowledged Caesar's power and named him dictator for life. Usually Roman dictators were only appointed during emergencies and for a limited term.

Caesar immediately planned a military expedition to conquer the Parthian Empire (in present-day Iran). Cleopatra decided to go with him. She was paying for the expedition and wanted to make sure Egypt got its share of the profit from it. His departure date was set for March 17. But his enemies had other plans.

A Great Betrayal

On March 15, 44 BCE, Caesar was murdered on the steps of the Senate. The plot to kill him involved at least sixty men, but the two who did the deed were Brutus and Cassius. According to Plutarch, a Greek historian and biographer, he was stabbed twenty-three times. It would go down in history as one of the greatest betrayals of all time.

Caesar did not recognize Cleopatra or Caesarion in his will. Instead, his estate was left to a great-nephew, Octavian, who Caesar had declared his adopted son. There was also a line in his will naming guardians for any son that might be born to him. Cleopatra was about seven

Octavian

months pregnant at this point, and there was no doubt that the child was Caesar's. After his death, Cleopatra waited a few weeks before she left with her brother and her son. She was weighing her options. She might have considered staying and giving birth to a child in Rome, but Roman law stated that a child born to a foreign woman could not be considered legitimate. So she made the decision to leave.

Meanwhile, Mark Antony, who had been the second-in-command in Rome, took over Caesar's state duties, but Rome was moving toward civil war. On her way home, Cleopatra had to deal with her sister Arsinoe, who had gained power during Cleopatra's time in Rome.

Arsinoe was upset about Cleopatra's return to Egypt.

Arsinoe had found her way back to Egypt after Caesar had spared her life and exiled her, and she was now trying to take back control of Cyprus, which Caesar had given her.

Cleopatra successfully took control of Cyprus for herself, and had new coins made that showed her holding her newborn son. While Cleopatra was gone, it's believed that Arsinoe had found another man to pass off as Ptolemy XIII, miraculously returned from the dead, and had claimed the throne with him by her side. The plan failed, but Cleopatra was concerned that Arsinoe would start working with Ptolemy XIV, who was now about fifteen and probably wanted power. Ptolemy survived their trip to Rome, but he didn't last long after he got home.

Ptolemy XIV died of unknown causes sometime in the late summer 44 BCE. It is likely that Cleopatra poisoned him because she couldn't let him become an enemy, though no one knows for sure what happened. Cleopatra named her son Caesarion her co-ruler. Since he was three years

A coin with Cleopatra's head on it, 51-30 BCE

old, she now ruled Egypt alone, and had no need to look for a husband. The officials she had trusted in her absence proved loyal once she got back. The problems now facing her were not political, at least for a little while.

Soon enough, though, Egypt was drawn into the final Roman civil war.

The Julian Calendar

Caesar reformed the Roman calendar to match the Egyptian way of keeping track of time. "The change from the lunar to the solar calendar caused an uproar," wrote one scholar. Before, Roman priests were the ones who decided when extra days were added to the lunar year, and they used this power to manipulate political events. By changing to a set solar calendar, Caesar took away power from the religious leaders. This calendar became known as the Julian calendar after Julius Caesar.

Julian calendar

Octavian, Marcus Lepidus, and Mark Antony (at top) fought against Brutus and Cassius (at bottom).

CHAPTER EIGHT

CLEOPATRA MEETS MARK ANTONY

Two sides were at war in Rome: the Caesarians, who remained loyal to Caesar and his ideals at the end of his life, and the Republicans, who didn't like the way Rome had been going under Caesar. Octavian, Marcus Lepidus, and Mark Antony led the Caesarians. Brutus and Cassius, the two men who had murdered Caesar, led the Republicans.

Cleopatra had a tightrope to walk. She couldn't support either side too strongly,

Sculpture of Octavian

because she couldn't predict who was going to win. One of the Caesarians, Dolabella, sent one of his deputies to Egypt to take control of the four legions that were still in Alexandria, and she let them go without a fight. One of her governors sent ships to help the Republicans, allegedly without her knowledge. These confusing actions meant that when the Caesarians finally beat the Republicans at the Battle of Philippi in Macedonia during October 42 BCE, the Egyptian queen was in a tricky position, once again. The Caesarion rulers divided responsibility for the empire into three regions. Octavian remained in Rome, and Mark Antony had responsibility for the eastern portion of the empire, including the states and the allies, of which one was Egypt.

Antony was in Greece for the winter of 42–41 BCE, gathering money for an expedition to conquer Parthia and gaining a lot of attention and admiration. He made comparisons between himself and the gods. He was setting himself up nicely for the campaign against Parthia, but he knew he needed Egypt's resources and support—and he thought he had the upper hand on its queen.

Mark Antony and Cleopatra

Antony settled in at the port city in Tarsus, and sent word to Cleopatra, summoning her to a meeting with him. He needed to know whose side she was on since it had not been obvious during the war. She ignored several requests to meet him, though she probably always intended to go, and when she did arrive, it was in a spectacle for the ages.

The queen arrived at Tarsus in the royal barge, which had been gilded for the occasion. It had perfumed purple sails, and the queen sat under a gold cloth canopy, dressed as the

Cleopatra makes
a grand entrance.

goddess Isis. Boys dressed as Greek gods fanned her, and the crew of the ship was entirely female. They were dressed as sea nymphs and used silver oars to row. Antony had been holding a hearing in the marketplace, but his entire audience deserted him to run to the docks and watch Cleopatra's grand entrance.

Antony invited her to dinner, but she declined. She then asked him to dinner instead! She had turned the barge into a fairyland. Thousands of tiny torches had been tied to the ship's rigging. The plates and goblets were gold and studded with precious gems.

The food was extravagant, and tapestries with silver and gold thread in them decorated the barge. Antony was overwhelmed, and not just by the food. Cleopatra was twenty-eight years old and as beautiful and intelligent as ever. She delivered the final blow when she told him at the end of the meal that everything—the tapestries, the plates and goblets, even the couches—was his to take away. Two nights later, she did it again. On the fourth night, guests had to walk through a hall covered in rose petals that came up to their knees on their way to the banquet.

Antony was no match for Cleopatra's charms. She was connected to the gods, and he wanted that connection for himself. She was clearly willing to give him the resources he wanted. Cleopatra and Antony were also attracted to each other. They were young, ambitious, good-looking, and brilliant in their ways. Antony's hesitation regarding Cleopatra's unwillingness to take sides during the civil war was tossed aside when they realized their mutual attraction and the great use they could be to each other.

Portrait of Mark Antony

Mark Antony was a popular, fun-loving, and capable military leader. He had risen through the ranks under Caesar. He was young, good-looking, friendly, loyal, generous, and a gentleman. After Caesar became dictator, Antony was made Master of the Horse, second-in-command under Caesar. Unfortunately, his relationship with Caesar became strained because Caesar did not like the life he was leading in Rome. Still, Antony remained loyal to Caesar even after Caesar's death.

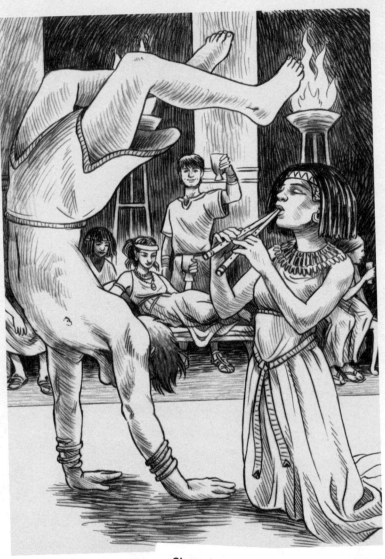

Cleopatra and Mark Antony
threw amazing parties.

CHAPTER NINE

BATTLE LINES ARE DRAWN

Cleopatra was a skillful and dedicated ruler. There were no large-scale revolts against her, and she was able to manage the enormous Egyptian government. But after Mark Antony returned to Egypt in 41 BCE, her reign became as much about pleasure as business. Cleopatra was delighted to have Mark Antony back, and she spent a lot of time and money entertaining him. Antony loved it.

The new, lighthearted Cleopatra took many

by surprise. She and Antony formed a group called "The Order of the **Inimitable** Life" or the Inimitable Livers. Along with a chosen few of the Alexandrian nobility, they devoted themselves to pleasure and food. They took turns throwing **extravagant** parties and banquets, all trying to outdo each other. Cleopatra spent a lot of time with Mark Antony doing all kinds of activities: athletic contests, festivals, gambling, contests, and sword fights.

The royal couple would also dress up as commoners and sneak out into the streets of Alexandria at night, and Antony sometimes anonymously picked fights with people just for the fun of it. The Alexandrians knew who they were, but didn't let on—they just made sure that Antony wasn't too badly hurt.

This behavior did not go down well in Rome. Cleopatra's reputation suffered even more than it already had. The Egyptian goddess seemed to

Cleopatra and Antony disguise
themselves as common people.

have stolen another good Roman man. Octavian, who was in Rome, wasted no time using the opportunity for his gain.

Duty Calls

In spring 40 BCE, the Parthian army started spreading out into present-day Israel and Jordan. Antony decided reluctantly that it was time to end his vacation and rejoin his troops in Syria. Cleopatra was pregnant with his child. Many of his former allies in the region and Republican troops loyal to Cassius's cause had joined up with the Parthian forces. His own troops were lost without his guidance, and hadn't been able to keep the Parthians back. Some of them started switching sides.

Foreign land in hieroglyphs

Even while he was trying to pull his troops together, worse news arrived from his wife, an ambitious woman named Fulvia. She wrote him that she was in Athens. She was forced to flee after she and Lucius Antonius, Antony's brother, had started a revolution against Octavian and failed. Antony raced to Athens.

Around that time, Cleopatra gave birth to twins. She named them Alexander Helios and Cleopatra Selene, giving her a son named for the sun and a daughter for the moon. Cleopatra basically disappeared from the historical record for the almost four years that she and Antony were separated.

Meanwhile, Octavian decided he wasn't up for a long battle with Antony. He probably assumed that Antony had nothing to do with the rebellion, and it wasn't worth risking civil war. Instead, the two leaders hammered out an agreement in which Octavian got Rome, Italy, and the parts of Gaul that Antony had controlled. Antony kept the eastern parts of the empire, and Marcus Lepidus would get Africa.

After Mark Antony's wife, Fulvia, died, Octavian suggested that Antony marry his sister, Octavia, in order to prove his commitment to the deal. She was shy, intelligent, unambitious, beautiful, loyal, and supportive. In many ways, she was the opposite of Cleopatra.

Antony accepted Octavian's suggestion and married Octavia. Octavia gave birth to a daughter in 39 BCE. Antony turned his attention back to the Parthian campaign, and was successful. Octavia joined Antony for part of his campaign but returned to Rome in fall 37 BCE. Antony headed to Antioch, a large city in the east that was in a very good location for political and military purposes. To the dismay of his advisers, he invited Cleopatra to meet him there. It appeared he was still in love with the Egyptian queen. But Antony had many reasons to reunite with Cleopatra. Egypt would be a powerful ally in future battles. Plus Antony wanted Cleopatra to take control of new territories taken from the Parthians.

Cleopatra ended up getting Cyprus, as well as territory and cities along the present-day Israeli-Syrian coast, and she seized Chalkis, an entire Arab kingdom. With that, she managed

Egyptian kings and queens could control time. The Egyptian dating system was continuous, much like ours, but reigns were dated from the year that the current throne holder took office— and they often restarted the dating on their reigns again when something good happened.

to reacquire most of the empire her Ptolemy ancestors had had in the third century.

Antony's favor for Cleopatra doesn't mean he neglected Roman interests. On the contrary, he was maintaining the most important territories in the eastern part of the Roman Empire. Egypt was one of Rome's closest allies in that part of the world.

Cleopatra joined Antony at Antioch, and that winter (37–36 BCE) was a second honeymoon for them. This time it was a working one, however. Antony was busy creating an army of one hundred thousand men to finish his defeat of the Parthian Empire. Cleopatra traveled back to Alexandria when the army left Syria.

By October 36 BCE, Antony was on the run after a siege of a city in ancient Iran went poorly for him. Getting back to Syria was difficult. His army was starving and tired, and only his strength of personality kept them all

Mark Antony
rallies his troops.

going through the mountains. He lost thirty-two thousand men. The survivors were in terrible shape, and he needed food, clothing, and money to keep the men from leaving. He sent word to Cleopatra, asking for help.

When she arrived in Syria, she had both relief and an infant to show him: Ptolemy Philadelphus. Once there, Cleopatra became a huge asset to Antony. She was used to running things, and so was able to manage her troops and his, leaving him free to focus on his military planning.

In the meantime, Octavian was proving to be a very successful ruler, both politically and

Father in hieroglyphs

militarily. This was of concern to Antony, since it upset the balance of power. Antony must have decided at this point that ultimate power lay with Cleopatra's help and support. Only with her behind him would it be possible to overthrow Octavian.

Octavia was on her way to meet Mark Antony with more troops. But his plans to overthrow Octavian meant he had to make a break with his wife, Octavian's sister. He sent a message telling her to send the troops on and go back to Rome. He did not want to see her. Octavian was delighted. When Antony's humiliated wife returned to Rome, he had to deal with the world's disapproval. Even some of his closest supporters had harsh words for him. Just as Octavian wished, Cleopatra was blamed. The public began to turn on Antony. In the meantime, however, Antony was still in Egypt.

Ruins on the
island, Samos

CHAPTER TEN

THE LAST PHARAOH OF EGYPT

Antony left Egypt in spring 34 BCE to take another crack at conquering more territory farther east. Cleopatra traveled with him, but turned back when they reached the Euphrates River. He went on to Armenia, and she went back to Alexandria.

Antony succeeded in his attempt to invade Armenia. When he returned to Alexandria, there was the routine Roman-style parade with the Armenian king on display in golden chains, and Antony hosted all the citizens in Alexandria to a huge banquet. He gave all his treasure to Cleopatra instead of to Rome, which angered the Romans.

Days later, Antony made matters worse by holding an enormous public ceremony in the great Gymnasium, an open-air sports stadium, calling the Alexandrian people to join him in recognizing Cleopatra and her children by their official titles and granting them territories in the name of Rome.

As the crowd looked on, Antony proclaimed Cleopatra the Queen of Kings, and her son Caesarion the King of Kings. He declared them the rulers of Egypt in the eyes of Rome. He then granted different regions of the empire to her other four children.

Feast in hieroglyphs

The ceremony, which became known as the Donations of Alexandria, didn't actually change anything. Most of the land Antony granted the Egyptian royal family was already under Egypt's control. But that's not how it played back in Rome. Octavian painted the Donations of Alexandria as a betrayal of Rome and Rome's interests, and the Senate refused to acknowledge Caesarion as Caesar's son.

Octavian and Antony began attacking each other verbally after this. Octavian also accused Cleopatra of wanting to rule Rome, of having ruined Caesar and now Antony. Both sides began preparing for open civil war.

Ready for War

In 33 BCE, Antony and Cleopatra went to the port city of Ephesus on the coast of the Aegean Sea. There, Antony began pulling his army together. Cleopatra sat in on meetings, gave advice, and made decisions. Antony's supporters were angered at her involvement, and begged him to send her back to Egypt. They claimed she was a risk to his image and that Octavian could use her as a wedge between Antony and the Roman

Samos, Greece

people. Antony did eventually order her to go home, but she convinced him to reconsider.

In spring 32 BCE, Cleopatra and Antony were at Samos, an island in the Aegean Sea. They split their attention between war preparation and feasts and parties in their honor. They then continued on to Athens and waited for the army.

Octavian wasn't having as much luck raising an army. He had to raise taxes to fund his own war preparations, and his popularity suffered horribly. If Antony had attacked in 32 BCE, he probably would have crushed Octavian. Instead, he stayed on the defensive, and Octavian was able to convince the public that Antony was disloyal to Rome.

In fall 32 BCE, Antony had succeeded in creating a sizable army and supply chain. He was ready for war. Back in Rome, Octavian was not. So he stalled by declaring war on Cleopatra alone, claiming that she wanted to take control over all Romans.

That bought Octavian enough time to get his troops in better position. In March 31 BCE, he was able to break Antony's supply chain and blockade the bay, trapping Cleopatra and Antony's fleet. Antony tried to draw Octavian into battle, but Octavian was settling in for a siege. All he had to do was wait for Antony's supplies to run out.

The Final Fight

As the summer stretched on, the strength and willingness of Antony's troops began to fade. At Cleopatra's urging, he decided to attack Octavian by sea. Prior to battle, he set fire to more than half of his own ships, as they could not be manned and he didn't want them to fall into Octavian's hands. But Octavian had the superior force with a fleet of four hundred ships.

Octavian and Mark Antony battle in the Ionian Sea.

Once the battle began, it was clear that Antony was outmatched. Octavian thought Cleopatra's money and valuable items might be on board Antony's ships. But Cleopatra's treasures were stored on a ship within her own fleet. When she saw a break in the fighting, her ships unfurled their sails and they made a run for it through the battling ships, fleeing south.

Antony turned his own ship to race after Cleopatra. Some of his fleet went after him, but many of his ships remained, and five thousand soldiers were lost. Antony's land army was convinced to give up. Their leader had abandoned them during the naval confrontation. Antony's fate was sealed. Losing that force gave him no other options. When Antony and Cleopatra got back to Alexandria, it turned out that Antony's allies and troops had all left or joined forces with Octavian. He sank into a deep depression, while Cleopatra responded to defeat with a rush of outlandish plans—trying to put a new military force together, thinking about running to Spain or India and setting herself up there. Eventually, Antony dusted himself off. They restarted their old partying ways. The new version of the Inimitables was called "Those Who Will Die Together."

It took almost a year for Octavian to come after them, due to tensions within his own ranks. As his forces drew closer, Cleopatra began stocking the tomb she'd built for herself with her valuables. She eventually moved into the tomb with her most closely trusted servants, Iras and Charmion. She didn't want to be taken alive.

Antony gathered what was left of his forces for a last stand against Octavian. He managed to drive the Romans back when they tried to enter Alexandria, and was able to come back to Cleopatra a victor one last time.

Cleopatra & Mark Antony Forever

On August 1, Octavian and his troops arrived in Alexandria again. Mark Antony assembled his remaining troops but suffered a miserable defeat as his men deserted him. When he received false information that Cleopatra had been killed, he stabbed himself in the stomach. He then learned she was not dead, and was taken to her tomb, where he was hauled up by ropes. The entrance to Cleopatra's tomb had already been sealed. Mark Antony died in Cleopatra's arms.

Octavian feared Cleopatra would burn her money or commit suicide, or maybe both. He had an aide go to her to try to calm her down. All she wanted was the promise that her children would be allowed to rule Egypt. The aide climbed in through window, but when she realized he was inside, she grabbed a knife and tried to use it on herself.

Mark Antony arrived at Cleopatra's tomb.

At first, Octavian didn't want Cleopatra to kill herself. He let her bury Antony's body. After his funeral, she fell terribly ill and stopped eating, saying she wanted to starve to death. Octavian threatened to execute her children if she didn't keep herself alive. Finally, Octavian went to visit Cleopatra himself. She convinced him she was willing to live for the good of her children. When she learned that Octavian was planning to leave for Rome, she decided it was time to act. Her beloved Egypt didn't belong to her anymore. She couldn't protect her children from the Romans.

A Noble Ending

Cleopatra asked to visit Mark Antony's tomb. Octavian allowed it. Cleopatra and her trusted servants, Iras and Charmion, went to his mausoleum, where his body was laid out, and she drank a toast to him. She wrote a letter to

Octavian, sealed it with her royal insignia, and sent it off to him by messenger.

He opened it, and found a request that she be buried next to Antony. He instantly sent troops to the mausoleum, but she was already dead, lying on a gilded couch with her rod and flail, the symbols of power for an Egyptian pharaoh, in her hands. Iras was dead at her feet, and Charmion was just adjusting the queen's crown. She told the guards that the act was fitting for a descendant of so many kings. Then she fell to the ground, dead as well.

Suicide in the face of defeat was a noble thing to do in the ancient world. It was viewed as taking control of one's destiny. The Ptolemies always had an affinity for poisons. It would have been very simple for Cleopatra's servants to get their hands on poisons, and she apparently had done a lot of tests of poisons on prisoners of war earlier in her reign, looking for one that killed painlessly.

Cleopatra

In the end, Octavian may have been relieved when Cleopatra died. He gave her a royal funeral, abiding by her wishes to be buried near Antony. Caesarion was executed—he was too much of a threat to Octavian's power. Cleopatra Selene was married off to a prince of a smaller African power. Alexander Helios and Ptolemy Philadelphus were sent off to be raised by Octavia.

Octavian ruled with absolute power in Rome after conquering Egypt. He might have conquered Cleopatra in war, but her story remains unbeatable. Cleopatra continues to fascinate the entire world thousands of years after her death.

10 THINGS YOU SHOULD KNOW ABOUT CLEOPATRA

1 People who disliked Cleopatra ended up writing a lot of the early history about her.

2 Although Cleopatra was certainly good-looking, it was her charm, wit, and beautiful voice that made her even more attractive.

3 Egyptian culture in Cleopatra's time allowed women to marry whomever they chose and manage their own businesses.

4 Cleopatra's ruling family, the Ptolemies, was notorious for their backstabbing and double-crossing ways.

5 It was very common for siblings to marry each other in ancient times, often in an attempt to consolidate family power and wealth.

6 In order to win over Julius Caesar, Cleopatra snuck into the royal palace in a sack carried by one of her loyal servants.

7 Cleopatra and Antony loved big parties and will go down in history as one of the most fun-loving couples of all time.

8 The society and the rules in Alexandria were more relaxed than in Rome. Octavian used this fact to turn Romans against Cleopatra and Antony.

9 Suicide was often viewed as a noble choice in ancient times, making Cleopatra's final act a fitting end to her life of greatness and defiance.

10 After Cleopatra's death, Egypt was ruled by the Romans, making her the last pharaoh of Egypt.

10 MORE THINGS THAT ARE PRETTY COOL TO KNOW

1 Roman, Greek, and some Alexandrian women (including Cleopatra) achieved their elaborate hairstyles with the help of a needle and thread! Their maids would style their hair into curls or braids and then sew them into place.

2 Egypt was the first civilization to develop beekeeping.

3 No contemporary paintings or images of Cleopatra exist, except the images of her in profile that appear on the coins she minted during her reign.

4 Cleopatra was very interested in medicine and in poisons. Some claimed she discovered a cure for baldness!

5 The 1963 film *Cleopatra*, starring Elizabeth Taylor, was one of the most expensive films ever made. In 2005, the cost of making it was adjusted for inflation, and it turned out to be more than $280 million dollars. Taylor was the first Hollywood star to be paid one million dollars for a role.

6 Two of the greatest English playwrights, George Bernard Shaw and William Shakespeare, have written plays based on Cleopatra's life.

7 Perhaps due to rising sea levels and earthquakes over many years, Cleopatra's Alexandrian palace is now underwater.

8 Cleopatra's full name was Cleopatra VII Philopator.

9 Cleopatra had massive amounts of gold and silver tableware, and it was a point of pride for her.

10 It could take as long as two and a half months to get from Alexandria to Rome in Cleopatra's time.

GLOSSARY

Empire: a group of countries or states that have the same ruler

Exile: to send someone away from his or her own country

Extravagant: very wasteful of money or resources

Famine: a serious lack of food in a geographic area

Gilded: Covered with a thin layer of gold

Inimitable: not capable of being imitated or copied

Legion: a unit in the Roman army consisting of 3,000 to 6,000 soldiers

Mercenary: a soldier who is hired to serve in a foreign army

Myth: an old story that expresses the beliefs or history of a group of people

Refuge: protection or shelter from danger or trouble

Successor: one who follows another in a position or sequence

Treason: the crime of being disloyal to your country by spying for another country or by helping an enemy during a war

Vulnerable: in a position or condition where a person or thing could easily be damaged

BIBLIOGRAPHY

Ancient World Leaders: Cleopatra, Ron Miller and Sommer Browning, Chelsea House, 2008.

Cleopatra: A Life, Stacy Schiff, Little, Brown and Company, 2010.

Cleopatra: Beyond the Myth, Michel Chauveau, translated from the French by David Lorton, Cornell University Press, 2002.

Sterling Biographies: Cleopatra, Egypt's Last and Greatest Queen, Susan Blackaby, Sterling, 2009.

INDEX